Encouraging Verses *of the* BIBLE *for* Christmas

75 Inspiring Meditations

Renae Brumbaugh

BARBOUR BOOKS
An Imprint of Barbour Publishing, Inc.

Published by Barbour Books, an imprint of Barbour Publishing, Inc., P.O.
Box 719, Uhrichsville, Ohio 44683, www.barbourbooks.com

*Our mission is to publish and distribute inspirational products offering exceptional value and
biblical encouragement to the masses.*

Member of the
Evangelical Christian
Publishers Association

Printed in the United States of America.

Introduction

There's no better time for gifts than the Christmas season! We all have treasured gifts we've received that hold special places in our hearts and holiday memories.

Do you treasure the Bible as a priceless gift? It's our answer for every question. . .our guide for life. It's powerful and everlasting. It's our hope and encouragement. It gives us meaning and purpose. It's God's Word, the very breath of Him. It is a gift that keeps on giving—available and applicable all day, every day, all year long.

The encouraging verses of scripture are truths that apply to every season of life. And in the season of Christmas, we can study and apply them in extra-special ways.

This Christmas, amid all the activity, be intentional and faithful to spend time in God's Word. Let this encouraging collection of devotions carry you through both the bustling moments and the calm ones to find the true meaning and joy of the season.

Merry Christmas!

The Daily Grind

*In the days of Herod, king of Judea, there was a priest named
Zechariah, of the division of Abijah. And he had a wife
from the daughters of Aaron, and her name was Elizabeth.*

LUKE 1:5 ESV

Zechariah and Elizabeth. They were born into a
religious world; both were descendants of Aaron, the
brother of Moses and the original high priest for the
temple. In the generations that followed, Aaron's
family retained the responsibility to care for the
temple and make sure things were as they should be.

It's only fitting they should be the parents of
John the Baptist, who would announce the presence
of the promised Messiah. They formed an important
piece of the puzzle, fitting seamlessly into place
to fulfill God's purpose. That purpose was, and
continues to be, to show His love in a dark world.

What if Zechariah and Elizabeth had rejected
their calling? What if they had said, "Meh. I'm not

really feelin' this whole ministry thing. I think I'll say no to God's purpose for my life and go join the circus."

If they had been disobedient to God's call, God's purpose would have been fulfilled. But Zechariah and Elizabeth would have missed out on the blessings of getting to play an important part in Christ's story. When we faithfully honor the daily grind commitments we've been given, God sees. He knows. And He chooses to honor those who honor Him.

A Blameless Life

They were both righteous in the sight of God, walking blamelessly
in all the commandments and requirements of the Lord.

LUKE 1:6 NASB

Zechariah and Elizabeth walked blamelessly in all
the commandments and requirements of the Lord.
Wow. That's a pretty impressive statement. But does
that mean Zechariah and Elizabeth were without sin?
Can any of us be truly blameless?

While none of us, apart from Christ, are
completely without sin, we can still be blameless.
Zechariah and Elizabeth were righteous people,
honoring God's commands. They were blameless,
meaning no one could charge them with any blatant
wrongdoing. They worked hard, showed kindness,
and lived with honesty and integrity. They didn't
cheat their bosses, they didn't gossip or slander, they
didn't manipulate things to get their way.

God knows our weaknesses. He knows our

limitations, and He doesn't sit behind some austere judge's desk waiting to smash us with His gavel at the first sign of stumbling. He's more like a coach, urging us to keep on, to keep fighting, and telling us what a great job we're doing when He sees we're doing our best.

Our goal should be to insert our own names in that verse: "(Your name) was righteous in the sight of God, walking blamelessly in all the commandments and requirements of the Lord." When we consistently do what is right and walk blamelessly, God is pleased.

Delayed Blessings

But they had no child, because Elizabeth was barren,
and they were both advanced in years.

LUKE 1:7 NASB

༄

The previous verse told us that Elizabeth and
Zechariah were blameless. Yet they were barren?
Children are supposed to be blessings from the
Lord. Why would God allow countless couples who
weren't nearly as righteous or blameless to have
a whole litter of children, while this one couple,
who served God with their whole hearts, remained
childless?

It happens all the time. We equate righteousness
with blessing. . .and though there is a correlation
there, sometimes God withholds the obvious
blessings because He has something even better in
store. God wanted John the Baptist to be an only
child, perhaps so his parents could pour all their
energy and training into him.

This isn't the first time God chose to bring a very special child into His story through a barren woman. Hannah begged for a child, and God gave her Samuel, who became a prophet. Sarah gave birth to Isaac, who in turn fathered the tribes of Israel. Rachel gave birth to Joseph, who saved Israel from starvation.

Our vision is limited to what's happening right now. When God withholds something we want, we often see it as a punishment. Instead, we need to trust God's eternal vision and know that He has something better waiting in the future. Like Zechariah and Elizabeth, our blessings will come, all in God's perfect time.

Startled

Then an angel of the Lord appeared to him, standing at the right side of the altar of incense. When Zechariah saw him, he was startled and gripped with fear.

LUKE 1:11–12 NIV

❧

Most of us would have been "startled and gripped with fear" if we saw an angel standing next to us. Imagine it. There was good old Zechariah, minding his business, doing his job, refilling the incense and making sure the altar was all clean and ready for worship when BAM! There's an angel. Right there.

Then again, Zechariah was at God's house. He was attending to God's business. Why was he surprised at all when one of God's own messengers showed up? Despite Zechariah's profession of faith, he didn't really expect God to show up. He didn't really expect miracles to happen. And when God did show up, Zechariah freaked out.

Zechariah is not alone. Most of us, despite our

professed faith, despite our declarations of belief in an almighty, all-powerful God, don't really expect anything unusual to happen. We go to church, but if God actually showed up there, we'd be startled. We might even feel afraid.

Like Zechariah, we need to adjust our way of thinking. When we call on God, we should expect an answer. Though He does like to surprise us at times, we should never be shocked when God shows up. Instead, we should wait expectantly for that moment when He does.

Just Wait

But the angel said to him: "Do not be afraid, Zechariah;
your prayer has been heard. Your wife Elizabeth will
bear you a son, and you are to call him John."

LUKE 1:13 NIV

"Your prayer has been heard." Wow. I wonder how many of us pray our perfunctory prayers without ever expecting them to be heard by the Almighty God. Sometimes prayer can be kind of like writing a letter to the president. We do it with a vague hope that it might be read, but we don't really expect a response.

Unlike the president, God doesn't have aides to read through His letters and send automated, preformulated replies. God personally attends to each and every attempt at communication with Him. He hears. He listens with interest. And He responds.

He cares when someone we love has cancer. He cares that we've lost our keys and we're late for work. Though He doesn't always answer the way we want

Him to, He always responds with love, moving us toward His perfect plan for our lives.

Zechariah and Elizabeth had surely prayed for many years for a child. They probably thought God didn't hear, or He didn't care. But God delayed His response for good reason: He had a very special child for them to parent, and that child needed to be born at a certain time. When God doesn't answer our prayers right away, we should wait. God hears, and He will answer.

Joy and Delight

"He will be a joy and delight to you,
and many will rejoice because of his birth."
LUKE 1:14 NIV

Sometimes God saves His greatest blessings for a
time when we're least expecting them. Zechariah
and Elizabeth had remained faithful in spite of
unanswered prayer. They chose to be content
without children. They trusted God and kept serving
Him, even if they didn't have any heirs.

Some of us might have lost faith or given up
hope. We might have become angry or bitter at God.
Perhaps Zechariah and Elizabeth questioned God, as
many of us would. It certainly isn't wrong to question
God; He welcomes our honesty. But in spite of the
fact that God didn't give them a child for so many
years, they never turned their backs on Him. They
chose to have faith, even when faith was hard.

And then one day an angel appeared, and

they learned they'd be parents. I wonder if God would have chosen them as the parents of this very special child if they'd traded in their faith for jaded hostility.

Probably not.

When things don't go your way, when God seems silent, hold on to faith in His goodness. One of these days, when we least expect it, God may grant our most cherished desires, bringing joy and delight to our hearts.

Grooming Our Hearts

*"For he will be great in the sight of the Lord. He is never
to take wine or other fermented drink, and he will be
filled with the Holy Spirit even before he is born."*
LUKE 1:15 NIV

The child the angel spoke of—John the Baptist—was
great in God's sight. But as far as the people of that
day were concerned, he was an oddball. Bats in the
belfry, out to lunch, mad as a hatter. . .take your
pick. If Zechariah and Elizabeth's boy had lived
today, he'd surely have been described as a lunatic.

After all, he lived in the wild. He ate bugs. His
hair was long and uncombed, and he dressed in
camel's hair. He probably didn't smell so great, either.

It's interesting how different our perspective can
be from God's perspective. The people we dismiss,
God may see as great. The people we think we're
above may actually surpass us in the kingdom of
heaven. After all, we look at things like name-brand

clothes, designer cologne, and expensive haircuts. We look at education and pedigree. God, on the other hand, looks at the heart.

While there's nothing wrong with wanting to look and smell nice, it should never be our primary concern. If we each spent as much time grooming our hearts as we spend grooming our bodies, we'd all probably be in better shape.

Coming Soon

"He will bring back many of the
people of Israel to the Lord their God."
LUKE 1:16 NIV

❧

Have you ever noticed how quickly Christmas gifts
lose their appeal? No matter how great the gift, by
the time Easter rolls around, the newness has worn
off. Our interest has waned, and we've moved on to
other things.

At this time in history, the Israelites had lost
interest in God. Imagine that! The God who had
rescued them time and again, the God who had saved
them from starvation, drought, and giants, who had
delivered them from slavery. . .He just wasn't that
exciting anymore.

Unlike a new car or a new gadget we may get for
Christmas, God loves us back. Though we may falter
in our devotion to Him, He never, ever loses interest
in us. That's why He sent Jesus.

He used John to build the suspense. "Get ready! Something big is about to happen," John told everyone. "The Messiah is coming soon!" John was the forerunner, the advertisement, the movie trailer for the big event: the coming of our Savior.

God loves us as much today as He did then. When we lose touch or drift away from Him, He finds ways to woo us back, to get our attention and help us fall in love with Him again. He wants to prepare us for the great things that wait in store because He loves us that much.

Impacting Eternity

*"And he will go on before the Lord, in the spirit and power
of Elijah, to turn the hearts of the parents to their children
and the disobedient to the wisdom of the righteous—
to make ready a people prepared for the Lord."*

LUKE 1:17 NIV

Elijah was perhaps the boldest, most faith-reliant
prophet in the Old Testament. He didn't speak with
diplomacy; he just said whatever God put in his
mind to say, without editing. Needless to say, that
didn't make him a popular guy.

But Elijah was faithful to God, and God was
faithful to Elijah. God promised that if Elijah would
be obedient, God would be there. He would help
Elijah. And God was true to His promises.

John had that same kind of faith. The message
he preached wasn't popular with the leaders of his
day. John was mocked for his convictions; he didn't
live an easy life. But his life was a productive one.

He impacted eternity. His faithfulness prepared countless hearts to receive Christ's message. They were more open to Jesus because John had already gotten them thinking in that direction.

God may ask us to do hard things, too. We may not always understand what God is doing, but we can be certain that God will never leave us. He will help us. And when we live our lives in faithful obedience, we may never know the impact we have on eternity.

The Beginning of Faith

*Zechariah asked the angel, "How can I be sure of this?
I am an old man and my wife is well along in years."*
LUKE 1:18 NIV

〰

Sometimes we forget who God really is. We want
Him to make sense in our human realm of reason.
But God can't be confined by human sensibility.
So when He chooses to work in a way that seems
illogical, we need to trust Him.

Zechariah was right; he and Elizabeth were too
old to have children. But if they hadn't been too old,
John would have been just another kid. It wouldn't
have been so obvious that God had His hand on
John's very existence. It was important that from the
moment of John's conception, people knew God
was involved in an unusual, special way. Perhaps that
caused people to listen a little closer to what John
had to say after he was grown.

God created us to use reason and logic, and

He expects us to use it. It keeps us on track and prevents us from doing foolish things. God is a God of reason, as well, and His laws are perfect and pure. They are the baseline for all human law and order. But unlike humans, God isn't limited to what makes sense. We must live within our own limits, but also trust that God isn't restricted like we are. That understanding is the beginning of faith.

Delivering Good News

The angel said to him, "I am Gabriel.
I stand in the presence of God, and I have been
sent to speak to you and to tell you this good news."

LUKE 1:19 NIV

Imagine having God's very own messenger deliver a personal message from the Almighty Himself! Zechariah must have felt special, amazed, and overwhelmed all at once. He probably didn't know how to respond.

Now, we are called to be God's messengers. Like that angel, God wants us to share His good news with those around us. Instead of telling them they'll have a baby, we're to tell them they are loved. They are special. And the God of the universe wants to have a close relationship with them.

Like Zechariah, people may feel overwhelmed at this message. They may not know what to do or say at such a revelation. But we don't have to worry about that. What they do with such a message is between them and God. We're just the messengers.

Oh, some may reject the message. It is pretty unbelievable, after all. But some will accept it. Just as that angel answered to God for delivering the message he was sent to deliver, we answer to God, too. He's commissioned us to share His love with others. God has given us a job to do, and He will reward those who do it faithfully and well.

When God Speaks

"And now you will be silent and not be able to speak until the day this happens, because you did not believe my words, which will come true at their appointed time."

LUKE 1:20 NIV

This seems a little harsh. After all, if an angel of God showed up at my workplace with a personal message from the Almighty, I'd probably be a little doubtful at first, too. Why would God take away Zechariah's voice for several months just because he was a little freaked out?

Yet, Zechariah was called by God. He was a minister, a priest in the temple. If anyone should have known and believed in the power of God, it was Zechariah. When God places us in positions of leadership and authority, He expects more of us.

As we grow in our maturity as Christians, God will place more and more responsibility on us. We may be asked to teach a class or mentor a younger

Christian. We may be put in situations where it's clear we're supposed to share our faith. It's an honor to be allowed to serve God in these ways, but with great honor also comes great responsibility. We have a job to do, and that job is to share His love. When we doubt God, we shake the faith of those around us who look up to us.

We can learn from Zechariah's mistake; when God makes Himself known, we should respond in faith, not doubt.

Have Patience

*Meanwhile, the people were waiting for Zechariah
and wondering why he stayed so long in the temple.*

LUKE 1:21 NIV

I wonder who was waiting for Zechariah. Some of them
had probably come to offer their sacrifices or pay their
alms, and they needed the priest to oversee things. They
had stuff to do. Places to go. People to see.

Perhaps a few of them had come to truly worship
and pray. They needed to talk to God, and in those
days, they had to go through a priest. They waited
and waited, thinking, "Come on, Zechariah! I really
need you, old buddy!"

Who knows? Maybe Elizabeth was in the crowd,
waiting for her husband so she could ask if he wanted
fish or lamb for dinner. All we know is that people
were waiting. They were wondering. And if they
were like many people today, they were probably
speculating.

"Maybe he's drunk. You know how the priests are with that communion wine."

"I wonder if he fell down. Maybe we should check on him."

Sometimes, things don't go as quickly as we'd like. Our plans get delayed, and we become impatient. But unlike our agendas, God's plans are perfect, and He is always right on time. Next time we become frustrated that He's taking too long, we can rejoice. There's a good chance He's working to bring about something great.

Making Sense of It All

When he came out, he could not speak to them.
They realized he had seen a vision in the temple,
for he kept making signs to them but remained unable to speak.

LUKE 1:22 NIV

I imagine there was quite a stir when Zechariah finally came out from behind the curtain. This was one of those moments that, if played out on the big screen, might win somebody an Academy Award. His eyes were round, his skin was pale. And his wrinkled hands waved around everywhere, trying to explain—without words—what had just happened.

I wonder if some of them thought he was finally going senile. Or maybe he'd had a stroke or a heart attack. If something like that happened today, we'd surely try to explain it away. There's always a logical reason for these things, after all.

But sometimes, God can't be explained. He is God, and His ways are higher than our ways. Just as I can't really explain advanced trigonometry to a two-year-old, there are some things about God that are simply beyond my comprehension. That doesn't mean trigonometry isn't a valid study, and that doesn't mean God's ways aren't legitimate.

His thoughts are often too advanced for my simple mind to grasp. But I can always trust His goodness. Zechariah was finally going to have a son. And when something happens that I don't understand, I can relax, knowing God has good things in store for me, too.

Completing the Task

When his time of service was completed, he returned home.
LUKE 1:23 NIV

 ⌒⌒⌒⌒⌒

Zechariah had a tragic experience. He'd seen an angel,
doubted God's Word, and now he was dumbstruck.
He couldn't speak. Most of us in Zechariah's shoes
would have written a note to our boss, packed up, and
gone home.

Not Zechariah. He'd been given a job to do.
His muteness didn't keep him from lighting incense
and fulfilling his duties as a servant of God. If he
had left, someone else in the temple would have
had to take up the slack. Perhaps there was no one
else. So he stayed. He worked. And when his job was
completed, he went home.

Sometimes, in the face of tragedy, the best thing
we can do is keep going. Keep performing those
tasks God has called us to do. Perhaps Zechariah's
muteness allowed him to really think about what

God was saying to him. Perhaps the sameness of his routine allowed him to get through without falling apart.

The work to which God calls us, however mundane it may seem, is a blessing and a gift. While there may be times when it's appropriate to leave a job unfinished, we need to make sure we're not jumping ship at the least sign of trouble. When we honor our commitments, it's healing to us, and it leaves those who watch with a good impression of what it means to be a Christian.

Keeping Silent

After these days his wife Elizabeth conceived,
and for five months she kept herself hidden.

LUKE 1:24 ESV

❧

Can you imagine Elizabeth's excitement when she
learned she'd finally have a child? In Jewish culture,
it was a shame if a woman couldn't produce children.
After all, God had promised Abraham that his
descendants would be as numerous as the stars. Any
woman who couldn't contribute to that promise
might feel like a failure. But now, in Elizabeth's
old age, God was finally blessing her! She probably
wanted to broadcast the news to everyone.

Yet she didn't go out and tell people right away.
Perhaps she didn't want to be the constant subject
of questions and gossip and rumors when she wasn't
even showing yet. She probably wore big tunics and
loosened her belts until it was so obvious that she
couldn't keep the news a secret any more. Perhaps

she used that time to think and pray and privately worship and thank God for remembering her.

When God speaks to us, sometimes it's good to savor the information for a while. When He's ready for others to know something, He'll make it clear to them as well, and we won't have to defend what we already know to be true. Proverbs 17 tells us that a wise man spares his words, and even a fool is thought wise if he keeps his mouth shut. Often, wisdom dictates that we hold our tongues, just as Elizabeth did.

He Did It!

"The Lord has done this for me," she said. "In these days he has shown his favor and taken away my disgrace among the people."
LUKE 1:25 NIV

Often when we pray, we expect the desired answer to our prayers to come right away. We want our loved one to be healed of cancer. Now. We want relationships to be fixed. Right now. We want a better job, a nicer home, a newer car. . .right now. Some of those prayers may seem nobler than others, but God wants us to come to Him with all our desires, no matter how important or trivial they may seem.

But asking for stuff is the easy part. Waiting for it is hard. Just as a child can't wait for Christmas morning, we figuratively tap our feet and bounce up and down, impatiently wanting God to deliver right away. But Christmas morning will eventually come, along with the gifts. And God will always, always answer our prayers.

He loves us, and He delights in giving good things to those who love Him with all their hearts. But His plans for us are bigger than we can imagine. Just as Zechariah and Elizabeth wanted a child—any child—God had in mind for them a very special child. And He has very special plans in mind for each of us, as well. We need to trust Him and be patient. He will deliver in His time.

Genealogy

In the sixth month the angel Gabriel was sent. . .
to a virgin betrothed to a man whose name was Joseph,
of the house of David. And the virgin's name was Mary.
LUKE 1:26–27 ESV

In the Old Testament, it was foretold that the Messiah would come from David's lineage. In Matthew 1, both Joseph and Mary are mentioned in the lineage traced back to David. Many scholars believe the genealogy in Luke 3 lists Mary's, not Joseph's, lineage. So either way, Jesus' lineage could be traced to David's.

It was unusual for a woman to be included in a genealogy listing, but in Matthew 1, there are four other women listed: Tamar, Ruth, Bathsheba, and Rahab. Of these four, Ruth and Rahab were Gentiles, Bathsheba was an adulteress, Tamar was a woman of questionable character, and Rahab was a prostitute. And that's not to mention David himself, who was an adulterer and a murderer.

It's a common misconception that God can only use those with spotless histories. We can see here that simply isn't true. God chose to bring His Son into the world through a line of misfits and sinners. In other words, Jesus became one of us.

Satan wants us to focus on our pasts and what we're ashamed of. But God sent Jesus so we could look to the glorious future He has for each and every one of us, no matter what we've done or where we've come from.

Like Mary

And he came to her and said, "Greetings,
O favored one, the Lord is with you!"

LUKE 1:28 ESV

How special Mary must have felt, to be singled out and called "favored one." I wonder what made her special. Was she particularly beautiful or kind or spiritual? The truth is that we don't know a lot about Mary. She was young, she was from David's lineage, and she was Jesus' mother. That's pretty much it.

But we do know that God's favor lies with each of us when we seek Him and long to please Him. Proverbs 3:3–4 tells us that if we hold fast to love and faithfulness, we'll find favor with God and man. In other words, when we make it a practice to love others and trust God, we'll find favor.

So from this, we can safely assume that Mary loved selflessly and that she sought God's wisdom and trusted His plan for her life. As we seek to find God's favor, we can look for ways to love those around us. We can consult His Word for wisdom, and go to Him often in prayer. And we can trust that no matter what comes, God loves us and has a good plan for our lives. Have faith. Love others. When we do those things, we, like Mary, will find favor with God.

Greatly Troubled

But she was greatly troubled at the saying,
and tried to discern what sort of greeting this might be.
LUKE 1:29 ESV

Mary didn't understand what was going on. She was "greatly troubled." That's probably the reaction most of us would have had, under the circumstances.

Yet the very thing that troubled her was, in fact, the blessed sign of a new beginning. She was concerned because she was confused, but God had in store for her one of the greatest adventures anyone has ever encountered. And while that adventure held many sorrows, it also held tremendous joy and blessing. Mary had been chosen by God to be the mother of His child.

God created us to have emotions, and He's not surprised or disturbed when we react with appropriate concern. He's not bothered by our questions. What disappoints Him is our lack of faith and our failure to trust Him.

Sometimes life confuses us, and we don't understand what's going on. It's not a sin to be concerned, or even greatly troubled, as Mary was. The sin comes when we choose to dwell in that place of anxiety. When we feel perplexed and baffled, wondering what in the world God is doing, it's okay. We can just take a deep breath, remember that God sees the big picture while we only see today, and remind ourselves that we can always trust God's love for us.

God's Favor

And the angel said to her, "Do not be afraid,
Mary, for you have found favor with God."
LUKE 1:30 ESV

❧

We often equate God's favor with success and blessing, with grassy meadows and fragrant flowers. But Mary knew much heartache. Her neighbors gossiped about her and said she got pregnant out of wedlock. Her fiancé nearly left her. She had to flee her home for a time, to protect her young Son from being murdered. And once He reached adulthood, that same precious Son was executed like a common criminal.

If that kind of life comes with God's favor, most would say, "Uh, no thanks, God. I'm fine on my own."

God's favor doesn't always bring immediate gratification. It does, however, bring higher joys than we could ever imagine. Mary played an intricate part in bringing salvation to the world. Generations have called her blessed. She watched her Son conquer death and ascend into heaven, and she got to point at Him and say, "That's my Son."

We must always keep in mind God's vision is for eternity and that our time here is but a breath. When we earn God's favor on earth, we will reap some of the rewards here. But many of the rewards will take place in heaven. A life lived in God's favor brings a rich inheritance of experience and blessing that can't be found outside of His will.

The Name of Jesus

*"And behold, you will conceive in your womb
and bear a son, and you shall call his name Jesus."*

LUKE 1:31 ESV

The name Jesus is a variation of the name Joshua,
which means "the Lord saves." Just as Joshua helped
save the Israelites in the Old Testament, Jesus would
come once and for all to offer salvation from eternal
doom. He also came to offer salvation from a life
filled with regret.

Oh, we all have regrets. We all wish we could
go back and do things differently. But with Christ,
we have a fresh start. While Satan would keep us
shackled to the past, Christ rescues us from our past.
He saves us from having to go back and second-guess
ourselves and our choices.

With Christ, we can look forward to a fulfilling
future. We have been rescued from sin and poor
choices. We're not defined by things that have already

happened. Jesus is our hero, carrying us into a beautiful future as long as we start today, right now, following Him.

Jesus. There is power in that name. The muscle of it isn't locked away in some never-never land that we can't access until we die. He saves us today and provides a way to find peace and contentment this minute, this hour, and every moment for the rest of our lives. All we have to do is trust Him, accept His power, and live by His wisdom.

The Throne

"He will be great and will be called the Son of the Most High.
And the Lord God will give to him the throne of his father David."

LUKE 1:32 ESV

Old Testament prophecies that the Messiah would
be given David's throne caused a lot of confusion.
David was a great king, the greatest king Israel had
seen. Naturally, the Israelites expected God's Son
to reclaim that earthly throne and bring Israel to
significant power again.

But the throne God referred to was far more
powerful than David's rule. Jesus would be king, yes.
But while David's reign was limited in boundaries
and influence, Christ's reign would have no limits.
All heaven and earth succumb to His authority, both
now and for eternity.

His throne is in heaven, yes. But He has
multiple thrones here on earth, from which He rules
in power. Those thrones are within me and you and

every person who steps aside and allows Him to be in control.

And while David's influence on earth was vast, it can't touch the impact we can have when each of us allows Christ to sit on the throne of our hearts. When we allow Him complete dominion over our words, thoughts, and actions, we become tools through which He impacts the people around us, and through them, we impact the world.

Never-Ending Friendship

*"And he will reign over the house of Jacob forever,
and of his kingdom there will be no end."*

LUKE 1:33 ESV

Most kings have an end to their earthly reign. Either their son or grandson (or daughter or granddaughter) takes over the throne, or someone overthrows their rule, or their country decides to do away with the monarchy. But Christ's rule is uncontested, and it is eternal.

Now, if we lived in the same house, in the same room, on an intimate level with the king or queen of any country, we'd have some pretty serious influence. Any ruler knows the value of a trusted, loyal friend and will go to great lengths to guard that friendship. The same is true for us! When Christ lives in our hearts, when we show Him that we love Him and are loyal to Him, He will protect us. He will bless us. He wants to give us the desires of our hearts.

The King of kings, the King of all Eternity, longs for our friendship. He invites us into an intimate relationship with Him. Why in the world would we ever turn down that kind of opportunity? Every day His invitation is re-extended. He yearns for our company, our conversation, and our constancy. He will never leave us. Why would we ever leave Him, even for a moment?

Questioning God

And Mary said to the angel,
"How will this be, since I am a virgin?"
LUKE 1:34 ESV

Mary was betrothed to Joseph. She was a virgin, but she wasn't uneducated about such things. She knew how babies were made. And she knew she hadn't done *that.*

Yet her question didn't reflect doubt as much as a desire for clarification. I can imagine what was going through her mind. "Um. . .God? With all due respect. . .how exactly is this going to happen? Exactly what am I supposed to do?"

Faith doesn't always have to be blind. Having faith means believing God can do anything. But God welcomes our questions, as long as they are asked with humility and trust.

It's often through our questions that our faith is strengthened. Our questions open up opportunities for God to answer and to reveal Himself in ways we never considered before. Mary didn't say, "Well, that's crazy. How in the world is that going to happen?" There was no sarcasm or doubt in her questions. . . only a sincere desire to better comprehend.

When we're faced with situations we don't understand, we can always feel free to ask God what's going on. We just need to ask those questions with humility and trust God, no matter how He chooses to answer.

Overshadowed

And the angel answered her, "The Holy Spirit will come
upon you, and the power of the Most High will overshadow you;
therefore the child to be born will be called holy—the Son of God."
LUKE 1:35 ESV

The Holy Spirit has always been around. He was
involved in the creation of the world (Genesis
1:2), and now played an intrinsic part in Christ's
conception. Gabriel told Mary the Holy Spirit
would overshadow her—in other words, He'd
surround her completely—and would cause her to
carry God's Son. Sounds incredible. Then again,
so does the creation story.

But for those of us who believe, who have
experienced God's presence in our lives, there's
nothing incredible about it. God is God, and He
will work in the way He chooses. The Holy Spirit has
been up-close-and-personally involved with humans
from the beginning, and He's just as intricately

woven into our world today.

However, the Holy Spirit is a gentleman. God gave us free will, and we have the choice to invite Him into our lives or not. He won't force Himself on us. Before Christ's ascension, He promised to leave His Holy Spirit with us. The Spirit of God stands ready to overshadow each of us, at our invitation. Though Mary's job was unique, we each have our own special purpose in this life. When we surrender to the Holy Spirit and allow Him free reign in our lives, amazing things will happen.

A Sign

"And behold, your relative Elizabeth in her old age
has also conceived a son, and this is the sixth
month with her who was called barren."

LUKE 1:36 ESV

Sometimes God uses what's happening in our own lives to speak to others. And sometimes He uses what's happening in someone else's life to speak to us. In this case, Mary was overwhelmed at the news she had received, so the angel pointed her to Elizabeth. "See? You're not crazy. You're not the only one God is doing amazing things with. Look at Elizabeth!"

Elizabeth was far too old to have children and had long carried the shame of being barren. But now she was in her sixth month! God allowed Elizabeth and Zechariah to conceive at the exact time He'd planned, so their son, John, would be a little older than Jesus, and so Elizabeth's pregnancy could be used as a sign to strengthen Mary's faith.

When God allows extreme situations in our lives, it's not only for our benefit. He sees the bigger picture, and He wants to use our lives as an important piece of the puzzle. He wants to use His blessings to demonstrate His goodness. He wants to use our faith, even in hard times, to illustrate His sufficiency. When we question our circumstances, we need to remember that God may be using our path as an illustration of His character to strengthen someone else's faith.

The Greatest Miracle

"For nothing will be impossible with God."
LUKE 1:37 ESV

❧

This verse is perhaps one of the most oft-quoted
verses in scripture. Nothing is impossible with
God; therefore a virgin can give birth to God's Son.
Nothing is impossible with God, so that same Son
can overcome death, rise again, and even ascend into
heaven. We can name miracle after miracle and point
to this verse: Nothing is impossible with God.

We can point to miracles of old and miracles of
today and credit God. But the biggest miracle of all
is one we often forget. Ironically, it's the one that is
closest to home.

Yes, God can heal cancer, and sometimes He
does. Yes, He can see that our bills are paid and we
have what we need. Yes, He can open doors that we
thought were shut and deadbolted. But none of these
come close to the greatest miracle of all. In spite of

all I've done to break God's laws, in spite of all the times I've failed to meet His standards, He forgives me. Not only that, but He picked me up out of my mess, adopted me as His own child, and clothed me with robes and a crown. A Cinderella story? Yes. A miracle? Yes. But it happened. And it will happen again and again, for each person who receives Him. A far-fetched, rags-to-riches story? Of course. But remember: Nothing is impossible with God.

Anchored to the Rock

*And Mary said, "Behold, I am the servant of the Lord; let it be
to me according to your word." And the angel departed from her.*
LUKE 1:38 ESV

૮જી૭

There's no way Mary could have known the ups and
downs of the journey that awaited her. If she had,
I wonder if she would have turned down the job.
Probably not. After all, God knew her heart. That's
why He chose her.

It's difficult to take her words and apply them to
our own lives. "I'm Yours, Lord. Do whatever You
want." Oh, we may say the words, but if we really
knew we were walking into a hurricane, if we knew
we'd travel through incredible stress and heartbreak,
would we still surrender?

When we truly, totally submit to God, we set
out on an adventure fraught with extreme highs and
lows—at least in our circumstances. But Mary was
able to remain steady in the storms because her peace

came from God and resided in her heart. Though none of us want to go through hardship, we can face any difficulty with serenity. We can truly say, "Go ahead, do what You want, Lord." Though our circumstances may change, the peace of God remains with those who trust Him completely. Like Mary, we are anchored to the Rock that will never move, no matter how fiercely the winds may blow.

Do It Now

*At that time Mary got ready and hurried to a town
in the hill country of Judea, where she entered
Zechariah's home and greeted Elizabeth.*

LUKE 1:39–40 NIV

How many minutes and hours and days have slipped
by while we have the best of intentions to accomplish
this or that, and yet we never actually get the thing
done? Whether it's the desire to write a memoir or
call an old friend or fix the hole in the screen door,
it's human nature to procrastinate.

But Mary didn't sit down and contemplate all
that happened. She didn't lie on her back and look
at the clouds, thinking how she should really go
visit Aunt Beth and find out what was going on. As
soon as the angel left, she got ready and hurried to
Elizabeth and Zechariah's.

While there are certainly times when we should
take a moment to pray and consider a thing before

we act, there are also times when we should act immediately. When we've heard from God and we know what He wants us to do, there's no excuse for procrastination. In many cases, delayed obedience is actually disobedience.

Mary found great comfort and wisdom in Elizabeth's presence. When we delay our compliance to God's direction, we often forfeit the blessings He has in store. Like Mary, we should make quick obedience a policy and a habit. When God tells us to do something, we should do it now.

God's Presence in Us

When Elizabeth heard Mary's greeting, the baby leaped in
her womb, and Elizabeth was filled with the Holy Spirit.
LUKE 1:41 NIV

⌒⌒⌒

The presence of God does funny things to people.
In this case, even Elizabeth's unborn child was affected
by the unborn Christ, and Elizabeth was overcome with
the Holy Spirit. God's presence is that powerful.

In the centuries since this moment in history,
God hasn't changed. His presence still has a powerful
effect on any situation. Because He chooses to reside
within the hearts of those who believe in Him, we
carry His presence with us.

When we submit to God and allow His Spirit
to control us, the people around us are affected,
whether they realize it or not. Though they may not
consciously understand what's happening, something
in their spirit recognizes God in our spirit, and the
entire dynamic of the relationship changes.

If that person is also a follower of Christ, they will often feel a peace. Or if they are living in rebellion against God, they may feel conviction. If we interact with a person who is not a believer, they will feel His presence and either resist or be drawn like a magnet. As Christians, it should be our goal to be so filled with God's presence that when we walk into a room, people know someone good and loving and powerful is in attendance.

Filled to the Rim

In a loud voice she exclaimed: "Blessed are you among women,
and blessed is the child you will bear!"

LUKE 1:42 NIV

In Hebrew culture, "Blessed are you among women,
and blessed are your children" was a common
expression. If you wanted to compliment someone,
you'd say, "What a great woman your mother is, to
have such a wonderful child." It was praise both to
the person and to the mother of that person.

Elizabeth was already caught up in the coming
birth of her own child. She was old and barren, and
this blessing had never been spoken over her. Yet
she freely rejoiced with Mary, whose child would be
even greater than her own. There was no pretense or
jealousy—only a sincere acknowledgement of Mary
and the child she carried.

When we are filled with the Holy Spirit, as
Elizabeth was, there is no room for jealousy or

cattiness or unkind words. "Filled" means to the rim, flowing over. There's no space for anything else. When we allow ourselves to be truly filled with the Holy Spirit of God, we'll find those things that aren't of God get pushed out and discarded. Our words become encouraging and uplifting. Our actions are driven by love and peace. If we want to truly do away with the bitterness, anger, and sadness that often tries to control our hearts, we must allow ourselves to be full to overflowing with the Holy Spirit.

Why Me?

"But why am I so favored, that the mother of my Lord should come to me? As soon as the sound of your greeting reached my ears, the baby in my womb leaped for joy."

LUKE 1:43–44 NIV

Elizabeth knew she was in the presence of the Almighty God. Yet she couldn't explain it; she couldn't figure out why in the world God would stoop to her level and show up physically in her presence. She knew she was unworthy.

Elizabeth isn't any different from the rest of us. We aren't worthy to enter His presence. But that doesn't matter to God. He doesn't wait for us to be good enough to come and eat at His house. He shows up where we are, knocks on the door, and hopes for an invitation to spend time where we live.

Just as baby John leaped for joy at the Messiah's presence, we can leap for joy, too! Jesus' name, Emmanuel, means "God with us." God Himself, the

King of kings and Lord of lords, longs to be in our presence. He yearns to spend time with us and have a close relationship with us. Why are we so favored?

Simply because He loves us.

Instead of asking, "Why me?" we can just rejoice that He chose us. We should open the door, invite Him in, and cozy up to a close, loving relationship with the One who loves us more than anything.

I Believe

*"Blessed is she who has believed that the
Lord would fulfill his promises to her!"*
LUKE 1:45 NIV

⌒⌒⌒

Do we really believe God will keep His promises to us?

Uh, sure we do. We know that if we believe in
Christ, we'll go to heaven when we die. We know that
when all is said and done in this world, God wins.
But what about the promises that come closer to
home?

Do we believe He's working all things together
for good, for those who love Him? What about when
things aren't good right now? What about when
everything seems to be going wrong? Do we believe
He's busy working on our behalf?

Do we believe He wants us to have a good, peace-
ful life right here and now? Do we believe His power
lives in us, and we can draw on that power any time?

There is often disconnection between what

we say we believe and what we actually live out. But Elizabeth's words to Mary can be applied to each of us. "Blessed is he or she who believes the Lord will fulfill His promises." When we truly believe God, when our thoughts and actions reflect that heartfelt belief that He is good, He loves us, and He wants good things for us, we open the door to God's blessings on our lives.

Mary's Song

*And Mary said: "My soul glorifies the Lord and my
spirit rejoices in God my Savior, for he has been
mindful of the humble state of his servant."*
LUKE 1:46–48 NIV

~~~

It feels really nice sometimes just to be noticed.
Just to know that someone sees us, that someone
cares. At that time in history, women were expected
to do their duty. They did what they were told and
married whomever their parents chose for them. But
rarely would anyone of significance take notice of a
humble, unmarried woman. Mary's heart was huge
and her thoughts were deep. . .but no one knew.

Yet God knew. God knows each of us intimately,
and He is fascinated by our thoughts. He longs to
converse with us, hear our hopes, our dreams, and
our opinions. He longs to spend time with us. And
He longs to reward those who pattern their lives
after Him.

God looked at Mary and saw past the unassuming garments and stature. He saw her heart, her mind, her soul. He saw all the things that made her unique and special, and He took notice. When He looks at you, when He looks at me, it's the same. He takes His time and really sees who we are. He adores us, and He longs for a close, familiar relationship with each of us.

The Bigger Picture

"From now on all generations will call me blessed,
for the Mighty One has done great things for me—holy is his name."
LUKE 1:48–49 NIV

For a young girl, Mary was pretty wise. She had
already learned a lesson that many of us spend a
lifetime learning. She'd already mastered what many
of us never quite comprehend. Eternity is more
important than right now.

Here she was, chosen by God to be the mother
of His child. In the moment, she must have been
terrified. People would talk about her and say she
was impure. And she'd have to tell Joseph! He'd
probably leave her. She must have wondered if she'd
spend her life as a single mom, outcast and alone.

But it doesn't appear those thoughts were a big
concern to Mary. The Almighty God had chosen
her, and from then on, all generations would call
her blessed. She knew she was a part of something

much, much bigger than herself. Her love for God and her reverence for His purpose was enough to make her rejoice.

We can rejoice, too. Oh, we may not have generations calling us blessed. . .but we might. We can be certain, though, that God has a special purpose for each of our lives. We can have joy, knowing that the Mighty One wants to do great things in us and through us. Holy is His name.

His Mercy Extended

"His mercy extends to those who fear him,
from generation to generation."

LUKE 1:50 NIV

It's interesting that Mary spoke here of God's mercy. By most standards, her life wouldn't feel very merciful. She'd be gossiped about. Her infant son would nearly lose His life at the order of a deranged king. And later, she'd watch that precious boy of hers be mocked and stripped and beaten and crucified in the cruelest of deaths, like a common criminal. Many of us, under the same circumstances, would have become bitter.

But Mary knew that through her, God would show His mercy to all generations. None of us deserves to have a relationship with the Creator of the universe. None of us meets His standards of holiness. But God had mercy on us, knowing we could never, ever live up to His standard. Our sins had earned us death, and we had no means of escape.

Jesus came to pay that death-price for us, so we wouldn't have to. It's kind of like if we had a gazillion traffic tickets and couldn't afford the fines, and our rich uncle paid them for us. Only, it's much more significant than that.

Through Christ, God showed His mercy. When we honor and revere God in our lives, that mercy gets extended to us. He sent Christ, not just so we wouldn't have to die, but so we could live.

Inconvenient

In those days Caesar Augustus issued a decree that a census
should be taken of the entire Roman world. (This was the first
census that took place while Quirinius was governor of Syria).
And everyone went to their own town to register.

LUKE 2:1–3 NIV

In those days, the census was taken every fourteen
years. The government didn't make it easy or convenient. Joseph was a good, upstanding citizen, and
he did what his government asked him to do. He
traveled many days with his pregnant wife over a long
distance so he could register his family.

Today, we live in a world of convenience. We
have cell phones and high-speed internet. Yet we still
balk sometimes at the things that are required of us.
As Christians, we must be faithful, not only in our
church commitments, but in every commitment God
has placed on us. We must remember that people are
forming their opinions about God by watching what
we do.

Sometimes it's not convenient to do the right thing. God requires us to do what is right anyway. Whether it's driving within an absurdly low speed limit or taking the time to properly report our taxes, God will notice our choice to live honorably. When we make righteousness a habit, we earn the respect of other people and the blessings of God.

Royal

So Joseph also went up from the town of Nazareth in Galilee to Judea, to Bethlehem the town of David, because he belonged to the house and line of David. He went there to register with Mary, who was pledged to be married to him and was expecting a child.

LUKE 2:4–5 NIV

ᔥᔤᔢ

Most kings inherit their positions from their earthly fathers, but Christ was King of kings before time began. The reign of an earthly king will come to an end, either because he gets too old or because someone forces him out of office. But Christ. . . Christ's reign will never end.

For centuries, the Israelites had looked forward to Christ's coming. They knew he'd be from the line of David, Israel's greatest king. They expected Christ, the Messiah, to lead their rise to greatness once again. They didn't understand that Christ wanted to rule hearts, not nations.

Though Christ is a different kind of king, he

was a descendent of David. And yet, David wasn't perfect. He loved God with all his heart, but he made some pretty major mistakes in his life. He committed adultery. He murdered. Still, God chose to graft David's genetics into His Son.

Think about that. The God of the universe, the King of kings, allowed Himself to be blended with the likes of a lowdown sinner. Though Christ is without sin, He is still one of us. When we accept Him, we become His family. That makes us royal.

Unexpected

While they were there, the time came for the baby to be born,
and she gave birth to her firstborn, a son. She wrapped him
in cloths and placed him in a manger, because there was
no guest room available for them.

LUKE 2:6–7 NIV

The manger scenes so artfully displayed on our
mantels make us smile. But as sweet as any child's
birth is, this birth wasn't glamorous or even sanitary.
During that time, stables were usually crude caves,
and the manger was more than likely a hollow place
carved into the rock wall where shepherds would
place food and hay. It was dark and stinky, and bits
of animal manure lay here and there. A far cry from
the sterile maternity ward at the local hospital.

The Israelites didn't expect their future king to
be born in a place like this. But God doesn't work
according to our expectations. He often comes to us
in a way that's the extreme opposite of what we would

expect. God's mind doesn't work like ours.

Just as the baby Jesus' presence lit up that dark, foul place, His presence in our lives today lights up the dark, smelly recesses of our hearts, where sin has taken over. When we open ourselves to the possibility that God may work in us in unexpected ways, that He may place us in undesirable situations in order to create something beautiful, we may be surprised at the things God chooses to do in our lives.

Blue-Collar Workers

And there were shepherds living out in the fields nearby,
keeping watch over their flocks at night. An angel of the
Lord appeared to them, and the glory of the Lord
shone around them, and they were terrified.

LUKE 2:8–9 NIV

⸎

Shepherding was a rough occupation. Because sheep
don't keep calendars, they need care seven days a week.
This meant shepherds were in constant violation
of the Sabbath laws. In order to be a shepherd, one
didn't have to have a high level of education. Though
shepherds were hard workers, they were at the bottom
of the societal ladder. They certainly weren't wealthy
or powerful. By today's standards, they might be called
"blue collar" or "rednecks." Not exactly the influential
group we'd expect the King of the universe to include
in His inner circle.

Yet it was to this group that God chose to make
His grand debut! God has always found more value

in humility than in self-righteousness. He'd rather make His home among people who know their place than with those who would compete for His place.

Whether we are high society or backwoods, wealthy or poor, God sees our hearts. He cares more about our souls than our status. And He longs to reside in people who humbly acknowledge their hopeless state, who won't hesitate to allow Him to sit on the throne of their hearts.

Great Joy for All People

But the angel said to them, "Do not be afraid.
I bring you good news that will cause great joy for all the people."

LUKE 2:10 NIV

~~~~~

The Jewish people had waited a thousand years for this prophecy to come true! At last, the Messiah had come. This was good news, indeed.

That news brought great joy for all people. We were separated from God by our sin. But no more! We have a Savior. There is One who paid the price we couldn't afford to pay, so we could have a close relationship with our Creator.

There is such joy in knowing that no matter who I am, no matter my bloodline or my status or popularity, I am accepted by the One who made me. No matter my education or abilities, I am wanted. I am cherished. I am loved, just the way I am.

What great freedom lies in that understanding! Though others may exclude or discard me, the King of kings longs to be near me. Though I may loathe myself, God thinks I'm beautiful. And truly, He knows my heart better than I do.

Yes, this is certainly good news. Yes, it brings great joy, great relief. I have a Savior. He loves me more than my limited mind can ever comprehend or imagine. And He will never, ever change His mind.

The Family Business

A thousand years before this happened, David had
a good friend named Barzillai. This friend was an
older man who helped David when he was in battle
and needed help the most. When David was ready
to go home, he asked Barzillai to go with him as a
helper and advisor.

Barzillai said, "No, David. I'm too old to be of
any help to you. Take my servant, Kimham, instead."
So that's what happened. Kimham went with King
David and served him well, and as a reward, David gave
him a little tract of land in the village of Bethlehem.
Kimham set up a family business there. . .Geruth
Kimham, or Kimham's Inn. It was a lodging place for
travelers.

That business stayed in the family, and a thousand

years later, God's Son was born there. It's an inspiring story, but it also makes me wonder about Barzillai. If he hadn't turned down the king's request and passed the job to someone else, perhaps Jesus would have been born in Barzillai's inn. Who knows? When we turn down opportunities to serve our King, we just might be turning down opportunities for great blessings—for us and for our descendants.

Hide and Seek

"This will be a sign to you: You will find a
baby wrapped in cloths and lying in a manger."
LUKE 2:12 NIV

⟡

Finding a baby wrapped in cloths wouldn't be hard.
It was Jewish custom to wrap a baby's abdomen in
cloths; it was believed to protect their internal organs
and keep them warm. Any newborn they found
would be wrapped in this way.

But finding a newborn baby in an animal's
feeding trough? Now that would be unusual. Even
low-income families would find a more appropriate
place to put their baby, unless the circumstances
were pretty extreme. . .like a family traveling far
from their home, in need of a place to stay and
finding nothing more than a cave used as a stable for
the local inn.

God wanted to make sure those shepherds found
His Son, so He made sure the circumstances would

be both unusual and extreme. The shepherds looked for Jesus, and they found Him. Jeremiah 29:13 tells us we will always find God when we look for Him with urgency and determination. Whether it's through signs, like a baby in a manger, or through His Word or another person's kind action, we will find Him. God doesn't hide Himself from those who sincerely seek Him. He makes His presence known in so many ways and waits for us to begin our quest. More than anything, He wants to be found.

And on Earth Peace

Suddenly a great company of the heavenly host appeared with the angel, praising God and saying, "Glory to God in the highest heaven, and on earth peace to those on whom his favor rests."

LUKE 2:13–14 NIV

᭡᭡᭡

At Christmastime we see part of this verse written on banners and Christmas cards and sung by choirs in shopping malls. "And on earth peace. . ." It's a beautiful sentiment, and one we all cling to during the holidays. But the promise isn't seasonal; it's eternal. And the promise isn't given to the entire earth. We often overlook that part of the verse. This assurance of peace is given to a specific group of people: those on whom His favor rests.

So how do we find favor with God? Isaiah 66:2 (NIV) tells us: "These are the ones I look on with favor: those who are humble and contrite in spirit, and who tremble at my word." When we humble ourselves before God, admit when we've messed up,

and really try to live our lives to please Him, God gives us peace.

As humans, we favor people we like. And we usually like people who also like us. God is no different! He favors those who favor Him, who long to spend time with Him, who praise Him and love Him with all their hearts. God delights in those who adore Him. They find His favor, and they have peace.

They Hurried

When the angels had left them and gone into heaven,
the shepherds said to one another, "Let's go to Bethlehem
and see this thing that has happened, which the Lord has
told us about." So they hurried off and found Mary and Joseph,
and the baby, who was lying in the manger.

LUKE 2:15–16 NIV

The shepherds didn't waste any time. They hurried
to follow through on this great VIP news tip. Was
the Messiah really here? Would they really have a
chance to lay their eyes on the Son of God? And, my
goodness, did somebody really put their baby in a
feeding trough?

The whole thing was unbelievable. But instead
of responding with skepticism, they investigated for
themselves. Sure enough, they found the angel's
words to be true.

God may not send a heavenly host to speak to us
today, but He still speaks to us very clearly through

His Word, through the Holy Spirit, and through the wisdom of godly people around us. Yet many times we shake off His messages as insignificant. Instead of jumping at the opportunity to seek Him further, we respond as skeptics and keep on about our business.

Though we shouldn't interpret every unusual event as a sign from God, we also shouldn't write things off just because they don't make sense. If we feel God is trying to tell us something, we should hurry to investigate further. He will always make Himself known to those who seek Him.

Talk About It

When they had seen him, they spread the word concerning
what had been told them about this child, and all who
heard it were amazed at what the shepherds said to them.

LUKE 2:17–18 NIV

❦

The shepherds were just plain old country folk. They
didn't have an advanced degree in political science
or a PhD. in rhetoric. God didn't ask them to change
who they were. He chose to reveal Himself to this
group of people for a reason.

The shepherds spread the word. They didn't
write lofty books or elegant poetry; they just talked
about what they had seen and heard. They told their
friends, neighbors, and family members what God
had shown them.

That's really what He asks us to do today. Many
times we keep our mouths shut about what God has
done in our lives because we think we might not
say it right. We hold quietly to our faith and leave

preaching for the preacher.

But God created each of us exactly the way we are for a reason. He doesn't want to change our personalities; He simply wants us to talk about Him. He wants us to tell the people around us, in our own words, about the beautiful things He has done in our lives. He loves everyone, but not everyone knows that. Like those shepherds, we are God's messengers, and our job is to spread the word.

Precious Memories

But Mary treasured up all these things
and pondered them in her heart.

LUKE 2:19 NIV

It's pretty standard for friends and family to get
all worked up about a new baby. Every mother
remembers special things about her child's infancy.
But when a bunch of strangers come around, asking
to see the baby and claiming a bunch of angels told
them He was God's Son. . . Now that's some pretty
special stuff.

Though Mary had found favor with God, she still
had some pretty tough roads to travel. Her life would
bring much heartache as she watched her beautiful
boy get accused of things He'd never done, then later
get publicly stripped and beaten until He was nearly
dead, only to be forced to carry a heavy wooden
cross uphill. She watched her Son as soldiers drove
nails through His hands and feet, mocked Him, and

placed a crown of thorns on His head. During that dark time, all she had to cling to was her faith that her baby was also God's Son.

When God does amazing things in our lives, it builds our faith. Each time He answers a prayer or opens a door, we need to store those memories in our hearts. Later, when times are difficult, we can draw on those treasured memories to get us through.

Changed

The shepherds returned, glorifying and praising
God for all the things they had heard and seen,
which were just as they had been told.

LUKE 2:20 NIV

Wow. What had started out to be just a normal, hum-drum night had certainly turned into an incredible experience! A birth announcement complete with an angel messenger and songs from the heavenly host, followed by a trip to town to see the long-awaited Savior. It was definitely a night to remember.

The shepherds eventually had to return to their normal lives. There was work to be done, sheep to be tended, bills to be paid. But when they returned, they were changed. They took their experience with them, and when they went back to work, they glorified and praised God for all the things they had heard and seen.

Sometimes God does exciting things in our lives.

He speaks to us in a new way, or He reveals Himself in a surprising manner. It's exciting and thrilling and beautiful, and we feel refreshed and closer to God than ever before. Eventually, though, we have to return to real life. But we don't have to return the same way we left.

For anyone who has experienced a true relationship with Christ, we are never the same. We are new creations. Though our surroundings may not have changed, we can change them by glorifying and praising God and bringing His presence with us wherever we go.

Set Apart

On the eighth day, when it was time to circumcise
the child, he was named Jesus, the name the
angel had given him before he was conceived.

LUKE 2:21 NIV

It was tradition that every Jewish male be circumcised on the eighth day after his birth. This set him apart as Jewish. While the reasons are many and complex, two of the most common reasons for circumcision are to get rid of unneeded flesh and to help with cleanliness.

Though circumcision provided an outward sign that a person belonged to God's chosen people, Romans 2:29 tells us of another kind of circumcision. This kind is required for all believers, male or female, regardless of race or nationality. It is the circumcision of our hearts.

Christ came so we could get rid of the unneeded, fleshly things that cause us to stumble. He came so we could be made clean. But we must continue to care for this precious gift of salvation. Every day, we need to cut the unnecessary things out of our lives that lead us into bad choices. Every day we must make sure our lives and hearts are being kept pure. This is what sets us apart as His holy people, keeps us from being infected by sin, and frees us to enjoy the rich, abundant life He wants for His children.

Required by Law

When the time came for the purification rites required by the
Law of Moses, Joseph and Mary took him to Jerusalem to present
him to the Lord (as it is written in the Law of the Lord,
"Every firstborn male is to be consecrated to the Lord"),
and to offer a sacrifice in keeping with what is said in the Law
of the Lord: *"a pair of doves or two young pigeons."*
LUKE 2:22–24 NIV

The purification time required was for Mary, not
for Jesus. When a woman gave birth to a son, she had
to wait forty days before she could go to the temple.

It's important to recognize that Mary and Joseph
did everything they were supposed to do, according
to the law. Being the parents of God's Son didn't give
them any special privileges. They still had to obey the
earthly laws, and they did so with conviction.

Though we answer to God first, we are still
subject to the laws of our city, state, and nation. It's
not okay with God that we got a speeding ticket on

our way to church or that we failed to report our tax information correctly. God wants us to honor the authority of our government. When we don't, we open ourselves up to criticism, and people lose respect for us. It is by living an upright, pure life, free from blame, that we are able to point others to the God who loves them.

Making the Cast

Now there was a man in Jerusalem called Simeon,
who was righteous and devout. He was waiting for the
consolation of Israel, and the Holy Spirit was on him.

LUKE 2:25 NIV

Simeon must have been a pretty special guy. Though he didn't play a lead role in the birth of the Messiah, God made sure he was included in the cast list. We don't know much about him; some say he was one of the priests at the temple. But we do know the important things about Simeon. He was righteous and devout. And he was a man of faith.

If he was righteous, we know he was a man of high morals. He was good and kind, honest and trustworthy. He was also devout. His devotion wasn't just for show; it was sincere and heartfelt. Finally, he longed for the Old Testament prophecies of the Messiah to come true. He believed them so much that he waited. He expected. Simeon knew God keeps

His promises, and he anticipated the moment when those promises would be fulfilled.

Though we will never hold God's Son in our arms as Simeon did, God has a special place in His cast for each of us. When we live with high morals, heartfelt devotion to Him, and expectant faith in His promises, He will bless us.

Moved by the Spirit

It had been revealed to him by the Holy Spirit that
he would not die before he had seen the Lord's Messiah.
Moved by the Spirit, he went into the temple courts.

LUKE 2:26–27 NIV

❧

If a person has never truly been in love, it's hard for them to understand the feelings involved. The same might be said about the Holy Spirit. For those who don't have the Holy Spirit in their lives, it's difficult to understand the relationship between the Spirit and the believer. After all, couldn't anybody just make up whatever they wanted and say, "The Holy Spirit told me"?

But for those who believe in Christ and who have been given the gift of the Holy Spirit, we just know. The Holy Spirit is our comforter, our encourager, our guide. He gives us wisdom, and He will never tell us anything contrary to His Holy Word. And the closer our walk with God, the clearer the Spirit's voice becomes.

Because Simeon walked closely with God, the Holy Spirit had made him a promise: He'd see the Messiah before he died. So when Simeon felt an unmistakable urge to go to the temple at a time he normally wouldn't have gone, he obeyed. As we walk closely with our Lord, His voice will become clear. Though we should always weigh hunches against scripture, we should never disregard the whispers of the Spirit.

Quiet Answers

When the parents brought in the child Jesus to do for him what the custom of the Law required, Simeon took him in his arms and praised God, saying: "Sovereign Lord, as you have promised, you may now dismiss your servant in peace."

LUKE 2:27–29 NIV

God really does keep His promises. Sometimes we look for those promises to be fulfilled in glorious ways. We long for angelic messengers and skies filled with heavenly host choruses. But many times, God answers prayers in a much quieter way.

Simeon had a hunch that he needed to go to the temple that day, so he did. And there was a young family, dedicating their son as was required by Jewish law. They were just taking care of business. That morning when he got up, Simeon didn't know that this day was the day he'd waited for. No angels woke him from sleep. God didn't speak to him in a dream. It was just a feeling, and then, there He was. The Messiah.

Sometimes we wait and wait for God to do something great in our lives, and it feels like it's never going to happen. But we never know what lies just around the corner. It may appear through a showy miracle, but more than likely, God will answer our prayers through soft whispers and quiet occurrences. One day, we will look up and realize God has answered our prayers.

Freedom for All

*"For my eyes have seen your salvation, which you have
prepared in the sight of all nations: a light for revelation
to the Gentiles ,and the glory of your people Israel."*

LUKE 2:30–32 NIV

The Israelites were God's chosen people. They wore
that knowledge like a badge of honor, as most of us
would. So when they learned the Messiah had come
to help the Gentiles, too, they were a little confused.

Gentiles? Really? They were dirty. They ate
unwholesome things. They didn't wash properly,
according to God's standards. They were foolish,
ignorant sinners.

Yeah.

The truth is that every one of us is a dirty sinner.
God didn't come to rescue the elite or the gifted.
He came to offer freedom and hope and new life for
every person.

This is great news, because there's not a single

person in this world who doesn't have things they're ashamed of. We all have things we'd rather people not know about it, whether it's our temper, something in our past, or the fact that stress causes us to eat a tub of ice cream when no one's watching. God knows all of that, and it doesn't keep Him from loving us. He doesn't care about race, nationality, physical attractiveness, or even intelligence. He simply loves us. He sent Christ and the Holy Spirit to offer hope for all people. That includes every single one of us, no matter what.

Marvelous Love

The child's father and mother
marveled at what was said about him.

LUKE 2:33 NIV

Time and again, Mary and Joseph heard confirmation that this baby son of theirs was the Messiah. From Elizabeth's baby jumping in her womb at His presence, to shepherds searching Him out in the middle of the night, to Simeon making a grand proclamation about who He was, there was little room for doubt. Their son really was the Son of God.

God does the same thing today. He tells us He loves us in His Word. But He doesn't stop there. He reminds us of that love over and over again. Sometimes it's through a soft wind on a hot day, or by leading us to the perfect dress, on sale, when we need it, or by letting us catch a whopper of a fish when we were about to give up. He shows His love through a friendly smile or word of encouragement from someone. He gives us rest when we can't sleep. He hugs us with His love.

Sometimes we let those reminders of His love pass by without notice. But we should make it a priority to marvel at those things, like Mary and Joseph did. When we pay attention, we'll find He sends unmistakable, inarguable evidence of His devotion to us. After all, His love for us is truly marvelous.

Worth It?

Then Simeon blessed them and said to Mary, his mother: "This child is destined to cause the falling and rising of many in Israel, and to be a sign that will be spoken against, so that the thoughts of many hearts will be revealed. And a sword will pierce your own soul too."

LUKE 2:34–35 NIV

In a popular song, the singer says to let her know if "the high was worth the pain." When we're in the middle of those gut-wrenching, painful times, we may wonder if the Christian life is worth it. I wonder if Mary felt that way as she watched her innocent Son die a criminal's death. In that moment, it must have felt like a knife pierced through the deepest part of her.

We must remember when we choose to live this Christian life that we haven't gotten to the high place yet. When it's over, we'll be able to look back and say whether or not it was worth it. We're still in the middle of the journey.

Oh, we'll have some wonderful highs and

gut-wrenching lows on this voyage. But when it's done, we'll have an eternity of nothing but highs. Nothing but joy. Nothing but praises and peace and prosperity forever. I wonder if God looks at us with that knowing smile and says, "I know it's hard. But you can tell Me when it's over if the high was worth the pain." I feel certain it will be.

Where God Is

There was also a prophet, Anna, the daughter of Penuel,
of the tribe of Asher. She was very old; she had lived with her
husband seven years after her marriage, and then was a
widow until she was eighty-four. She never left the temple
but worshiped night and day, fasting and praying.

LUKE 2:36–37 NIV

By most people's standards, Anna didn't have much
of a life. She was married for seven years; there's no
mention of any children. Then she was widowed,
and she never remarried. She was a prophet, which
means she was regarded as an inspired teacher. For
a woman to be given the title of prophet, her gifts
and abilities must have been noteworthy. This also
shows that the Jewish people, God's chosen people,
didn't discriminate against women as much as other
cultures of the day.

It says she was at the temple all the time, fasting
and praying. This is probably a figure of speech—
meaning Anna was at the temple every chance she

got, serving Him, talking about Him, praising Him. God may not call us to be at the church all the time, but He does want us to be present with Him in our thoughts, words, and actions. When we make it a priority to be where God is, He will show up in amazing ways.

Tell Everybody

Coming up to them at that very moment, she gave thanks to God and spoke about the child to all who were looking forward to the redemption of Jerusalem.

LUKE 2:38 NIV

༄

Talk about being at the right place at the right time. When we spend our days with God, praising Him, serving Him, and allowing His Spirit to guide us, we will always be at the right place at the right time. Anna spent her life serving God. She stayed at the temple, encouraging and inspiring people with her words as much as possible. And one day she saw God's Son, face-to-face.

Just think. Her entire life, God had been preparing her for this moment. Every step of her existence had led her to this place, where she would get to look in God's sweet baby eyes, hear Him coo, and touch His soft skin. And then she told everybody who would listen about her experience.

God doesn't require us all to be gifted prophets. He only wants us to stay near Him so we can experience the great things He has planned for us every day. When we stay close to Him, we'll see and touch His presence in an authentic, life-changing way. Then He wants us to talk about those experiences, sharing His love and kindness with everyone who will listen.

Due Diligence

When Joseph and Mary had done everything
required by the Law of the Lord, they returned
to Galilee to their own town of Nazareth.

LUKE 2:39 NIV

~~~

When choosing the people who would raise His
Son, God didn't draw names out of a yarmulke.
He specifically chose a man and woman who would
faithfully, consistently keep His laws, who lived
quiet, upright lives, and who honored Him in all
they did. Joseph and Mary did everything required
by law. No bypasses or shortcuts. If God said to do
something, they did it.

Other than that, they lived a simple, quiet life.
They returned to the small town of Nazareth, where
Joseph worked as a carpenter. He didn't try to move
his business to a larger city to make more money. He
didn't get distracted trying to become richer or more
powerful. Joseph and Mary were content to work

hard, love each other, and serve God.

Sometimes we get sidetracked, chasing down dreams that, in the long run, aren't really that important. We have grand goals for our careers or our lives, and we want to take shortcuts to get there. But true fulfillment can't be found in shortcuts or bigger paychecks. It can only be found by diligently honoring God and being content with where He's placed us. It is in that kind of God-honoring constancy that we will find our greatest fulfillment.

Wise Men

After Jesus was born in Bethlehem in Judea, during the time of
King Herod, Magi from the east came to Jerusalem and asked,
"Where is the one who has been born king of the Jews?
We saw his star when it rose and have come to worship him."

MATTHEW 2:1–2 NIV

The Magi went to a lot of trouble just to deliver some
baby gifts. They traveled thousands of miles. There
were no jets or SUVs to make the journey quicker.

Why did they do it? The answer is in scripture.
They came to worship the one who was born King
of the Jews. They're called wise men for a reason:
they had wisdom to know this was one King worth
knowing. They went because, somehow, they knew
who Jesus was. He was God's Son.

Unfortunately, today we often take a different
approach. Instead of seeking God, we wait for God
to find us. Instead of giving Him gifts, we want Him
to bless us. But isn't God worth seeking, no matter

the price? Shouldn't we give Him everything we have, simply because of who He is?

When we seek Him, we will find Him. When we give to Him, He will give back until our cups and hearts overflow. We can never out-give God, but it sure is fun to try. Like the Magi, we can all be wise men and women when we spend our lives chasing God and giving Him the best we have.

Unfounded Fear

When King Herod heard this he was disturbed,
and all Jerusalem with him.
MATTHEW 2:3 NIV

When Herod heard there was a new king on the horizon, he was concerned. And he had reason to be; he wasn't the proper heir to the Jewish throne. He wasn't a descendant of David, and it would be easy for someone from that line to overthrow his power with the Jewish people.

But Herod didn't have any cause for concern. Christ didn't come to take Herod's throne. Instead, He gave His life for Herod. If Herod had only known, he might have joined the Magi on their journey. If he had known, he could have bowed down to the King of kings, as well.

Sometimes we resist God because we're afraid He'll take something from us. But God loves us. He is generous and kind. He doesn't want to take good

things from us; instead, He wants to make our lives better.

Because we see things from our limited human perspective, at times it may seem like God is taking the things that are most precious to us. But anything He takes away will be replaced by something so much better. When we examine our hearts, we may find a Herod-like resistance to God's plan. But we can replace that fear with faith that He wants to pour out His goodness on our lives.

Preconceived Notion

When he had called together all the people's chief priests and
teachers of the law, he asked them where the Messiah was to be
born. "In Bethlehem in Judea," they replied, "for this is what the
prophet has written: 'But you, Bethlehem, in the land of Judah,
are by no means least among the rulers of Judah; for out of
you will come a ruler who will shepherd my people Israel.'"

MATTHEW 2:4–6 NIV

The religious leaders of that time were aware of the
prophecies. They knew the Messiah would be born
in Bethlehem. But they wanted an earthly king to
restore Israel as a superpower. They didn't have any
use for a spiritual king. So when Christ came, they
rejected Him and became His greatest enemies.

God always keeps His promises. But sometimes
we have preconceived ideas about what we want
those fulfillments to look like. We may ask God for
a new job, but instead, He may help us succeed in
our current job. We may pray for healing; He may

use our sickness to teach us things that will give us healthier spirits.

God may not always show up the way we expect Him to. But when we call on Him, He will answer. We just need to make sure we're looking for Him and not for our idea of what He's supposed to be.

Dirty Rotten Liar

Then Herod called the Magi secretly and found out from them the exact time the star had appeared. He sent them to Bethlehem and said, "Go and search carefully for the child. As soon as you find him, report to me, so that I too may go and worship him."

MATTHEW 2:7–8 NIV

⟳

Because of this trick, Herod went down in history as a murderous liar. He didn't want to worship Jesus; he wanted to kill Him. But he was afraid the wise men wouldn't help him if they knew the truth, so he lied.

Herod felt the end justified the means. In his case, neither the means nor the end was good. In life, we're faced with opportunities to do what we think is best. Sometimes we think it's okay to fudge a little. To tell little lies, or cheat here and there, to achieve what we feel is the right end.

If Herod had trusted God, he would have known Christ wouldn't hurt him. He could have rested easy despite news of a newborn king. When we trust God, we can be at peace, even when the future looks bleak. We don't need to relax our ethics or twist the circumstances to have things work out; if we leave things to God, they will always work out well for us in the end.

Follow the Star

After they had heard the king, they went on their way,
and the star they had seen when it rose went ahead of
them until it stopped over the place where the child was.
MATTHEW 2:9 NIV

Those men traveled a long, long way. Their journey was tiresome, to be sure. Traveling in those days was difficult. And that star just kept moving and moving and moving. There were probably moments when they wanted to give up and go home.

Such is life, isn't it? The journey is long and difficult. Sometimes we want to turn around and go back. Back to a time when life seemed easier. Back to a time when things were more fun. Back to a place where it was simple.

But the journey is worth it! Just as the wise men followed the star, we can follow our Lord with confidence that He will lead us to an incredible destination. Though it seems the path grows longer and longer, we can still follow with assurance that we'll end up at the wonderful place God has planned for each of us from the beginning of time. Not only do we have amazing things in store, but we have a loving, compassionate, and fun traveling companion—for our Lord has promised to walk with us each step of the way.

Overjoyed

When they saw the star, they were overjoyed.
MATTHEW 2:10 NIV

After many months of travel, the star finally stopped.
The wise men must have wondered if they were
seeing things. Could this be it? Could their journey
be coming to an end? If so, what would they find?

After checking their calculations to make sure,
they realized that yes, the star was actually, finally
standing still. The long-awaited moment was at
hand. They'd finally get to see this newborn king
with their own eyes.

We don't know exactly who the wise men were.
Some say they were learned men from other cultures;
they had studied prophecies and studied the stars,
and they knew something big was going on in the
universe. But whoever they were, their hearts were
filled with joy to learn their journey hadn't been in
vain. They had remained diligent, they had followed,

and now they would reap the reward.

One day soon every believer will experience that kind of excitement. When we remain diligent in following God, when we don't give up and don't turn back, we will eventually reap the rewards of such faithful pursuit. One day our star will stop, and it will catch us by surprise. We'll look around and see that we've arrived at the fulfillment of one of God's promises. And we will be overjoyed.

Expensive Gifts

On coming to the house, they saw the child with his mother Mary,
and they bowed down and worshiped him. Then they opened their
treasures and presented him with gifts of gold, frankincense and myrrh.

MATTHEW 2:11 NIV

⚜

Jesus was probably a toddler by the time the Magi
arrived. When they saw Him, they immediately bowed
down and worshiped Him. They could see what some
others of that day could not: Christ was worthy of
worship simply because He was God's Son, and not
for anything He had done for them at that point.

Part of their worship was to give Him valuable
gifts. Gold was fit for a king, frankincense was a gift
for deity, and myrrh was a spice used when someone
died. Many have speculated that these gifts gave Mary
and Joseph the financial resources to flee to Egypt
and later relocate in Nazareth.

As part of our worship, we need to give our most
valuable gifts to God. Whether it's our time, talents,

or money, God is worthy of our very best. Just as the Magi's gifts were used for something important, God will take our gifts (when given in true worship) and use them to reap an eternal harvest. And the great thing about God is that we can't out-give Him. When we invest in Him, the return on that investment is always abundant.

Change in Plans

And having been warned in a dream not to go back to Herod,
they returned to their country by another route.

MATTHEW 2:12 NIV

The Magi had made a long, difficult journey to see Jesus. But God told them to go back a different way so Herod wouldn't demand they help him locate the Messiah. But going back the way they'd come was most likely the easiest route. After all, they were already familiar with the stopping points. They'd been on the road a long time; they were probably anxious to get home.

When we choose to obey God, He may lead us in a different direction than we expected. That change in plans may not make sense at first. It's always easier to stay with what's familiar; change is hard. But obedience to God is always in our best interest. If the Magi had disobeyed, Herod would have forced them to help him, or killed them if they refused. God was protecting them and protecting His Son.

Though following God may lead us on some unexpected paths, we can be sure that obedience is always the best route. Even if we don't understand what He's doing at the time, we can trust that eventually His plan will be made clear. And His plans for us are always made with absolute love for us in His heart.

Clear Direction

When they had gone, an angel of the Lord appeared to Joseph
in a dream. "Get up," he said, "take the child and his mother
and escape to Egypt. Stay there until I tell you, for Herod
is going to search for the child to kill him."

MATTHEW 2:13 NIV

This was the second time God spoke clearly to Joseph
through an angel in a dream. Each time, the angel
gave Joseph well-defined instructions. While Joseph
wasn't Jesus' biological father, he was Jesus' earthly,
adopted father, and he was responsible for the care
and safety of his family.

It might have been tempting for Joseph to dismiss
those dreams as nonsense. Everybody has dreams.
They don't all mean something so significant. But
Joseph was a godly man. He had a close relationship
with the Holy Spirit. He surely prayed daily and asked
God for wisdom and guidance, and he was sensitive to
God's leadership.

God offers guidance to those who are receptive to His leadership. He gives wisdom and direction to those who ask for it. Sometimes we may not even know we need to ask for something specific—Joseph didn't know at this time that Herod planned to kill his child. But because Joseph's relationship with the Father was consistent and strong, God showed him what he needed to know at the time. He will do the same for each of us when we consistently seek Him and listen for His voice.

Out of Egypt

So he got up, took the child and his mother during the night
and left for Egypt, where he stayed until the death of Herod.
And so was fulfilled what the Lord had said through
the prophet: "Out of Egypt I called my son."

MATTHEW 2:14–15 NIV

There's a curious parallel between this flight to
Egypt and the previous one in the Old Testament.
In Genesis we learn how Joseph's brothers sold
Joseph into Egyptian slavery. Those same brothers
later fled to Egypt for help from the famine.
Joseph, who had earned a position of authority in
Egypt, was able to save the young nation of Israel
from starvation. Centuries later, God (through
Moses) led the Israelites out of captivity, back into
the Promised Land.

Here, Mary and Joseph take Jesus to Egypt for
safety, but He later comes back to lead all people out
of the captivity of sin. Now the story extends to each

of us. Just as God called the Israelites out of Egypt and provided a way of escape, just as He called His Son out of Egypt, He calls us. Through Christ, we have a way out from the sin that holds us hostage. But He won't force us to leave. He invites, He leads, but the final decision to stay or escape is up to each of us.

Madman

When Herod realized that he had been outwitted by the Magi,
he was furious, and he gave orders to kill all the boys in Bethlehem
and its vicinity who were two years old and under, in accordance
with the time he had learned from the Magi.

MATTHEW 2:16 NIV

Herod was so afraid Jesus wanted to take something
away from him—his throne—that he went insane
with fear and fury. Imagine ordering the deaths of
countless infants, all in the name of job security!
Poor Herod. The realization of what he'd done must
have stolen his sleep for the rest of his life.

Sometimes we sense God is doing something
unexpected, and we're afraid He wants to take something from us. We get nervous and act irrationally.
At times we may feel we're going crazy trying to hang
on to something we want, because we can't imagine
life without it. But if we'd just relax and submit to
His direction, we'd learn what Herod never learned:

God loves us. His plans for us, though they may seem frightening, are always good. If we will let Christ rule our hearts, He will bless us in ways we can't imagine. And though His plans for us may look different from the plans we have for ourselves, they will always lead us to the peace and fulfillment that can only come from God.

Bitter Tears

Then what was said through the prophet Jeremiah was fulfilled:
"A voice is heard in Ramah, weeping and great mourning,
Rachel weeping for her children and refusing
to be comforted, because they are no more."

MATTHEW 2:17–18 NIV

Rachel was the favorite wife of Jacob. From Jacob's twelve sons came the twelve tribes of Israel. Rachel is given the symbolic title "Mother of Israel" and is pictured as she cries for her children. This quote is first found in Jeremiah, where she supposedly weeps for the Israelite captives. Now she weeps for all of the little baby boys who were killed.

This is just a literary way of encompassing the endless weeping of the Israelite mothers at the loss of their infant children. Anyone who has ever lost a child knows the pain and anguish of such a tragedy. There are no words to comfort a mother whose child has preceded her in death.

God must weep similar tears over us when we reject Him. Satan wants to destroy us, but God has done everything in His power to prevent that. He gave us the choice, however. We can choose His redemption or reject it. But when we refuse to accept His gift of salvation through Christ, we are actually choosing death. God loves us, and like Rachel, like those mothers, His heart is broken over our demise.

Legacy

*After Herod died, an angel of the Lord appeared in a dream
to Joseph in Egypt and said, "Get up, take the child and his
mother and go to the land of Israel, for those who were
trying to take the child's life are dead."*

MATTHEW 2:19–20 NIV

In 4 BC, Herod the Great contracted an incurable
disease and died. Scholars believe Jesus was between
one and two years old, which means Herod was
struck down soon after he demanded all the baby
boys be killed. Herod was so afraid one of those
babies would grow up and take his throne. Turns
out, it didn't matter anyway. He didn't live long
enough for anyone to take it away.

Would Herod have gotten this deadly disease
even if he hadn't ordered the death of innocent
children? Maybe. We will all die, at some point. If
Herod had concentrated on being the best ruler he
could be that day, instead of worrying and fretting

over something that might happen tomorrow, he would have certainly left behind a better legacy.

We never know what the future will bring, but God's Word tells us we're not to worry about tomorrow. If we take today as a gift and use every moment of it to live well and love well, we will leave behind a beautiful legacy that will last for generations to come.

The Man He Became

God made him who had no sin to be sin for us,
so that in him we might become the righteousness of God.

2 CORINTHIANS 5:21 NIV

❧

The story of Christmas is a beautiful one, filled with
warm fuzzy feelings of peace and goodwill. We see the
image of the infant Christ, and we're reminded that
God is a gentle God.

The infant in that manger grew to heal the sick,
feed the hungry, and give sight to the blind. He
endured false accusations. He was dragged to court
and accused, though no one really knew what He was
being accused of. He was cursed at, spat upon, and
beaten to a bloody pulp.

When He could hardly stand and the skin on His
back was raw, He was given a heavy, splinter-filled
cross to carry uphill to His place of execution. Then
a Roman soldier hammered heavy spikes through
His hands and feet. The crowd mocked and jeered

as a crown of thorns was placed on His head. And never once did He curse back, or spit back, or try to retaliate. He took it. He took our sin on Himself, because He knew it was the only way. He knew somebody had to carry that sin. So He carried it for us.

Because of that sacrifice, we can stand clean before God. This Christmas, as we view the infant Christ, let's not forget the man that baby became and what He did for us.

The Perfect Gift

For to us a child is born, to us a son is given, and the government
will be on his shoulders. And he will be called Wonderful
Counselor, Mighty God, Everlasting Father, Prince of Peace.
ISAIAH 9:6 NIV

So many Christmas gifts end up sitting on a shelf,
never to be used or opened. Many of them get
regifted the next year at another Christmas party.
These gifts, though well intended, are a waste. They
were often bought just because somebody needed to
bring a gift. But ultimately, they take up space and
gather dust.

Our favorite gifts are the ones we actually use.
God knew this, and He gave us the best gift ever
in Jesus Christ. He gave us a counselor, to consult
when we're not sure what to do. He gave us a loving
Father, for when we need a safe place to retreat
For those times when peace seems elusive, He
gave us the Prince of Peace. And for when we feel

overwhelmed, He gave us the Mighty God, who can move mountains with a whisper.

Why would we ever put such a gift on a shelf? God wants us to enjoy this present—our Savior, Jesus Christ—each moment of our lives. Today and every day, He offers us wisdom and peace and security and love through His Son. And it never runs out, either. The more this gift is used, the more abundant it grows.

Scripture Index

2 CORINTHIANS

Celebrate Jesus' birth with these great titles from Barbour Books!

Available wherever great Christian books are sold!